# BEAU PEEP BOOK 12

## From The
### DAILY STAR

© 1991
Express Newspapers plc,
245 Blackfriars Road,
London, SE1 9UX.
Printed by Grosvenor Press
(Portsmouth) Ltd.
Reproduction by
Cloverleaf
Communications Ltd.
Researched by
Terry Greenwood

ISBN 0-85079-234-7

£2.95

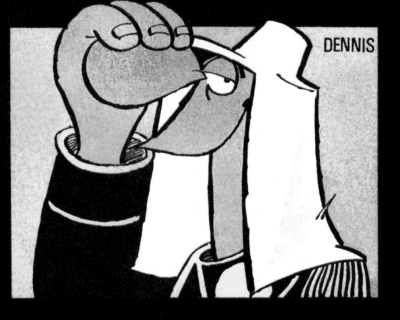

DENNIS

HAMISH

SERGEANT BIDET

COLONEL ESCARGOT

THE VULTURE

Roger Kettle (writer) and Andrew Christine
(artist) pause during a game of pool to think up
suitable nicknames. Following in the tradition of
Alex "Hurricane" Higgins, they will now only
answer to Andrew "Cool Breeze" Christine and
Roger "OO, It's A Bit Nippy" Kettle.

# THE ADVENTURES OF LEGIONNAIRE
# BEAU PEEP

FROM THE **Star** DAILY

THIS IS A NICE PLACE SO DON'T SHOW ME UP!

2983

I ALWAYS THINK A KNOWLEDGE OF DINING-ROOM ETIQUETTE SHOWS THAT A GENTLEMAN IS—

DON'T DRIBBLE ON THE CUTLERY, DENNIS.

WHAT ARE YOU HAVING TO START?

I DON'T KNOW.

2984

WHAT ABOUT A PRAWN COCKTAIL?

GOOD IDEA!

WE'LL GET STUCK INTO THE BOOZE AND TO HELL WITH FOOD!

MENU

I COULD DO WITH A HOLIDAY.

YOU KNOW, LIKE THOSE CAREFREE ONES WE USED TO HAVE AS KIDS.

WHAT, BEING SICK ON THE DODGEMS?

3018

SIGH! DO YOU REMEMBER YOUR CHILDHOOD HOLIDAYS?

YEP!

3019

BAREFOOT WITH MY BUCKET SPADE AND LITTLE FISHING NET!

I STOOD OUT A MILE IN MANCHESTER.

WHAT WAS YOUR FAVOURITE HOLIDAY DENNIS?

3020

I THINK THE TIME WE GOT THE TRAIN TO BLACKPOOL.

WHAT HAPPENED?

DAD PULLED THE CORD—WE WERE MEANT TO BE GOING TO BARNSLEY.

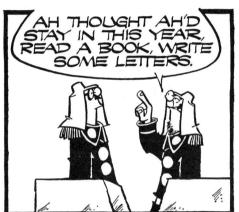

Panel 1: AHA! A NEW RECRUIT!

Panel 2: REMINDS ME OF MYSELF ALL THESE YEARS AGO!

Panel 3: EXCEPT, HE'S NOT CRYING AND THERE ARE NO TOENAIL TRACKS BEHIND HIM.

Panel 4: YOUR FIRST DAY IN THE LEGION, SON? / YES.

Panel 5: ER...SHOULD I CALL YOU "SIR"?

Panel 6: POOR LAD — HE THINKS I'M AN OFFICER!

Panel 7: YES, CALL ME "SIR" AND SALUTE!

Panel 8: ...AND THERE I WAS SURROUNDED BY THE ENEMY... / GOSH!

Panel 9: ...SO I KNOCKED OUT 30 OF THEM AND ESCAPED.

Panel 10: I GOT TEN MEDALS FOR THAT! / CAN I SEE THEM?

Panel 11: SORRY — I HAD TO EAT THEM ONE TIME I WAS LOST IN THE DESERT.

3186
3187
3188

D'YOU FANCY A GAME OF BLACKJACK?

WHAT ARE THE RULES?

I'VE GOT TO WIN.

3195

HAH! I WIN AGAIN!

HANG ON...

3196

...WHAT'S THAT ACE OF SPADES DOING UP THAT SLEEVE?

I'VE NO IDEA — IT SHOULD BE UP THIS ONE WITH THE REST.

IS THIS WHAT YOU'RE REDUCED TO — CHEATING AT CARDS?

A MAN WHO CHEATS IS A MAN WITHOUT DIGNITY!

THIS MAN WHO CHEATS HOPES YOUR BOTTOM EXPLODES!

3197

YAWN! THIS IS BORING.

I'M SURE ALL THIS WAITING AND WATCHING DAMAGES THE BRAIN.

YOU'LL PROBABLY FIND IT SORE WHEN YOU SIT DOWN.

3216

I KNOW— LET'S PLAY THE "YES-NO" GAME!

3217

BY ASKING QUESTIONS, I'VE GOT TO MAKE YOU SAY "YES" OR "NO."

HELLO.

YES?

LET'S PLAY FOR MONEY.

REMEMBER, DENNIS, IT'S A VERY EASY GAME.

3218

ALL YOU HAVE TO DO IS AVOID SAYING "YES" OR "NO."

IS YOUR NAME DENNIS?

YES.

HANG ON, THAT'S A TRICK... NO, MY NAME'S NOT DENNIS... WAIT... YES IT IS...ER... NO...

I DEMAND THE RIGHT TO CONDUCT MY OWN DEFENCE!

HOW CAN I PUT THIS IN LAYMEN'S TERMS WITHOUT RESORTING TO LEGAL JARGON?

YOU COULDN'T CONDUCT A BUS, FATSO!

3225

FINALLY TO MY SUMMING UP!

I REMIND THE COURT OF THE CROWN VS. McTAGGART, 1892.

WHAT HAPPENED THEN?

NO IDEA—I JUST LIKE REMINDING PEOPLE OF IT.

3226

THANK GOODNESS — IT'S DENNIS!

NOW YOU CAN SAVE ME FROM THIS MOCKERY OF A TRIAL!

IS THIS WHERE THE HANGING IS?

3227

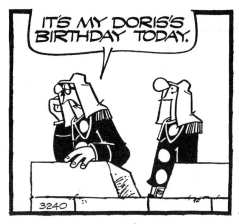

WE'RE BEING VISITED BY SOME TOP BRASS TODAY...

...SO I WANT YOU TO LAY ON A SPREAD AND USE THE BEST CUTLERY

NO PROBLEM, SIR!

WHAT'S "CUTLERY"?

KITCHEN

3108

WHAT AM I GOING TO DO?

3110

TWO HOURS TILL THE GUESTS ARRIVE AND ALL I'VE GOT IS SOME SALMON SOUP?

AND THAT'S GOT A BIT TO GO.

PLOP!

WHAT A DISASTER THAT MEAL WAS— EVERYTHING WAS BURNT!

THE SOUP WAS BURNT, THE MAIN COURSE WAS BURNT—EVEN THE ICE-CREAM WAS BURNT!

3113

I HAD TO POUR THAT OVER MYSELF—I WAS ON FIRE AT THE TIME.